Patty Sleem

WHAT THE BIBLE SAYS ABOUT...

Words that can lead to success and happiness

WHAT THE BIBLE SAYS ABOUT...

PREP Publishing
1110 ½ Hay Street
Fayetteville, NC 28305
(910) 483-6611

Grateful acknowledgement is made to the following for permission to reprint previously published material:

Library of Congress Cataloging-in-Publication Data
Sleem, Patty, 1948- Davidson 11.96 5/02
    What the Bible says about-- : words that can lead to
    success and happiness / Patty Sleem.
        p. cm.
    ISBN 1-885288-22-0
    1. Christian life--Quotations, maxims, etc. 2. Bible--
    Quotations.
    3. Large type books.
    I. Title.
BV4513 .S58 2001
220.5'2036--dc21
                                        2001021003
                                        CIP

Printed in the United States of America

Dedicated to my sons
Patrick and Kevin
on the eve of their graduations
from college and high school

and to my sister Bennie

I hope these words will be a source of
strength, hope, and guidance as they
lead lives filled with love, laughter, and faith.

For I know the plans I have for you,
says the Lord,
plans for welfare and not for evil,
to give you a future and a hope.
Then you will call upon me
and come and pray to me,
and I will hear you.

JEREMIAH 29: 11-12

FOREWORD

This book is intended to be a compilation
of favorite Bible verses
and not a comprehensive collection of
scripture on each subject. It is my hope that
these verses will make the Bible "come alive" to
people not familiar with the Bible and provide
comfort to those who have studied
the Bible and know its verses well.

Patty Sleem

WHAT THE BIBLE SAYS ABOUT...

Words that can lead to success and happiness

Also by Patty Sleem

SECOND TIME AROUND—a novel

"Author Patty Sleem has captured the essence of small town Southern life and the many layers of relationships one finds there. She skillfully weaves a picture of 'the way things are done' in small town politics and families. Various theories and clues lead the reader through a well-written mystery. Excellent detail helps the reader to both see and feel the scene. In one instance, you can almost smell the sea as described by the author."
—*Detroit DAILY NEWS*

BACK IN TIME—a novel
"Lots of contemporary issues in a plot that pulls readers through the pages. Glass ceilings in the ministry, sexual harassment, and homicide. Sleem develops an attractive character in Maggie Dillitz. Intriguing exploration of current Judeo-Christian issues."
—*THE BOOK READER*
Order from www.prep-pub.com

CONTENTS

What the Bible says about...

WHAT THE BIBLE SAYS ABOUT...

Words that can lead to success and happiness

Patty Sleem

What the Bible Says About...

Life and Living

And what does the Lord require of you but
to do justice, and to love kindness and
to walk humbly before your God.
MICAH 6:8

Thy word is a lamp to my feet
and a light to my path.
PSALM 119:105

Hope deferred makes the heart sick,
but a desire fulfilled is a tree of life.
PROVERBS 13:12

A man's mind plans his way,
but the Lord directs his steps.
PROVERBS 16:9

A cheerful heart is a good medicine, but a
downcast spirit dries up the bones.
PROVERBS 17:22

Many are the plans in the mind of man, but it is the purpose of the Lord that will be established.
PROVERBS 19:21

Behold, what I have seen to be good and to be fitting is to eat and drink and find enjoyment in all the toil with which one toils under the sun
the few days of his life which God has given him, for this is his lot.
ECCLESIASTES 5:18

Cease to do evil, learn to do good; seek justice, correct oppression; defend the fatherless, plead for the widow.
ISAIAH 1:17

In returning and rest you shall be saved; in quietness and in trust shall be your strength.
ISAIAH 30:15

He who is noble devises noble things,
and by noble things he stands.
ISAIAH 32:8

For we are his workmanship, created in
Christ Jesus for good works, which God
prepared beforehand, that we should walk
in them.
EPHESIANS 2:10

Thus says the Lord:
Take heed for the sake for your lives,
and
do not bear a burden on the sabbath day
or bring it in by the gates of
Jerusalem.
And do not carry a burden out of your
houses on the sabbath or do any work,
but keep the sabbath day holy,
as I commanded your fathers.
JEREMIAH 17:21-22

Thus says the Lord: Do justice and
righteousness,
and deliver from the hand of the oppressor
him who has been robbed.
And do no wrong or violence to the alien,
the fatherless, and the widow,
nor shed innocent blood in this place.
JEREMIAH 22:3

He who walks righteously and speaks
uprightly,
who despises the gain of
oppressions,
who shakes his hands, lest they hold a
bribe,
who stops his ears from hearing of bloodshed,
and shuts his eyes from looking upon evil,
he will dwell on the heights;
his place of defense will be the
fortresses of rocks;
his bread will be given him,
his water will be sure.
ISAIAH 33:15-16

For I know the plans I have for you,
says the Lord,
plans for welfare and not for evil,
to give you a future and a hope.
Then you will
call upon me and come and pray to me,
and I will hear you.
JEREMIAH 29: 11-12

Sow for yourselves righteousness;
reap the fruit of steadfast love;
break up your fallow ground,
for it is the time to seek the Lord, that he
may come and rain salvation upon you.
HOSEA 10: 12

Hate evil, and love good,
and establish justice in the gate.
AMOS 5:15

Let justice roll down like waters, and
righteousness like an everflowing stream.
AMOS 5:24

Seek the Lord, all you humble of the land,
who do his commands; seek righteousness,
seek humility.
ZEPHANIAH 2:3

This is the word of the Lord to Zerubbabel:
Not by might,
nor by power,
but by my Spirit,
says the Lord of Hosts.
ZECHARIAH 4:6

Render true judgements,
show kindness and mercy
each to his brother,
do not oppress the widow, the fatherless,
the sojourner, or the poor;
and let none of you devise evil
against his brother in your heart.
ZECHARIAH 7:9-10

A prudent man sees danger and hides himself;
but the simple go on, and suffer for it.
PROVERBS 22:3

These are the things that you shall do:
speak the truth to one another,
render in your gates
judgements
that are true and make for peace,
do not devise evil in your hearts
against one another,
and love no false oath,
for all these things I hate, says the Lord.
ZECHARIAH 8:16-17

All things are lawful for me,
but I will not be enslaved
by anything.
I CORINTHIANS 6:12

Bad company ruins good morals.
I CORINTHIANS 15:33

Unless the Lord builds the house,
those who build it labor in vain.
PSALM 127:1

You shall love the Lord your God
with all your heart,
and with all your soul,
and with all your mind.
This is the great and first commandment.
And a second is like it:
you shall love your neighbor as yourself.
On these two commandments
depend all the law and the prophets.
MATTHEW 22:37

There is nothing outside a man
which by going into him can defile him;
but the things which come out of a man
are what defile him.
MARK 7:15

Man does not live by bread alone…
man lives by everything
that proceeds out of the mouth of the Lord.
DEUTERONOMY 8:3

For everything there is a season,
and a time for every matter under heaven:
A time to be born,
and a time to die;
A time to plant,
and a time to pluck up what is planted;
A time to kill, and a time to heal;
A time to break down,
and a time to build up;
A time to weep, and a time to laugh;
A time to mourn, and a time to dance;
A time to cast away stones,
and a time to gather stones together;
A time to embrace,
and a time to refrain from embracing;
A time to seek, and a time to lose;
A time to keep, and a time to cast away;
A time to rend, and a time to sew;
A time to keep silence, and a time to speak;
A time to love, and a time to hate:
A time for war, and a time for peace.
ECCLESIASTES 3:1-8

A good name
is better than precious ointment.
ECCLESIASTES 7:1

Trust in the lord with all your heart,
and do not rely on your own insight.
In all your ways acknowledge him,
and he will make straight your paths.
Be not wise in your own eyes;
fear the Lord and turn away from evil.
It will be healing to your flesh
and refreshment to your bones.
PROVERBS 3:5-8

All flesh is grass, and all its beauty
is like the flower of the field.
ISAIAH 40:6

The grass withers,
the flower fades;
but the word of our God
will stand for ever.
ISAIAH 40:8

Thou who art of purer eyes
than to behold evil
and canst not look on wrong,
why dost thou look on faithless men,
and art silent
when the wicked swallows up the man
more righteous than he?
HABUKKUK 1:13

Give thy servant therefore an understanding
mind to govern thy people,
that I may discern between good and evil.
I KINGS 3:9

The measure you give will be
the measure you get.
MARK 4:24

The Lord loves those who hate evil.
PSALM 97:10

He who loves pleasure
will be a poor man;
he who loves wine and oil
will not be rich.
PROVERBS 21:17

The drunkard and the glutton
will come to poverty,
and drowsiness
will clothe a man with rags.
PROVERBS 23:21

All these things my hand has made,
and so all these things are mine,
says the Lord.
But this is the man to whom I will look,
he that is humble and contrite in spirit,
and trembles at my word.
ISAIAH 66:2

Seek the Lord and live.
AMOS 5:6

Wine is a mocker,
strong drink a brawler; and
whoever is led astray by it
is not wise.
PROVERBS 20:1

Even now the axe is laid
to the root of the trees;
every tree therefore that does not bear fruit
is cut down and thrown into the fire.
MATTHEW 3:10

Let your light so shine before men,
that they may see your good works
and give glory to your Father
who is in heaven.
MATTHEW 5:16

If your right eye causes you to sin,
pluck it out and throw it away;
it is better that you lose one of your members
than
that your whole body be thrown into hell.
MATTHEW 5:29

Do not be anxious about your life,
what you shall eat or what you shall drink,
nor about your body,
what you shall put on.
Is not life more than food, and the body
more than clothing?
Look at the birds of the air:
they neither sow nor reap
nor gather into barns,
and yet your Heavenly Father feeds them.
Are you not of more value than they?
And which of you
by being anxious
can add one hour to his span of life?
MATTHEW 6:25-27

According to your faith be it done to you.
MATTHEW 9:29

Behold, I send you out
as sheep in the midst of wolves,
so be wise as serpents
and innocent as doves.
MATTHEW 10:16

A sower went out to sow.
And as he sowed,
some seeds fell along the path,
and the birds came and devoured them.
Other seeds fell on rocky ground,
where they had not much soil,
and immediately they sprang up,
since they had no depth of soil,
but when the sun rose they were scorched,
and since they had no root
they withered away.
Other seeds fell upon thorns,
and the thorns grew up and choked them.
Other seed fell on good soil
and brought forth grain,
some a hundredfold,
some sixty,
some thirty.
He who has ears let him hear.
MATTHEW 13:3-9

He is a Jew who is one inwardly,
and real circumcision
is a matter of the heart,
spiritual
and not literal.
ROMANS 2:27

Let love be genuine;
hate what is evil;
hold fast to what is good.
ROMANS 12:9

Live in harmony with one another;
do not be haughty,
but associate
with the lowly;
never be conceited.
ROMANS 12:16

Let us pursue what makes for peace
and for mutual upbuilding.
ROMANS 14:19

Do not be children in your thinking;
be babes in evil,
but in thinking be mature.
I CORINTHIANS 14:20

You were called to freedom;
only do not use your freedom
as an opportunity for the flesh,
but through love
be servants of one another.
For the whole law is fulfilled in one word,
"You shall love your neighbor as yourself."
But if you bite and devour one another
take heed
that you are not consumed by one
another.
GALATIANS 5:13-15

There remains a Sabbath rest
for the people of God;
for whoever enters God's rest
also ceases from his labors
as God did from his.
HEBREWS 4:9-10

Do not neglect to do good
and to share what you have,
for such sacrifices are pleasing to God.
HEBREWS 13:16

See to it that no "root of bitterness"
spring up and cause trouble.
HEBREWS 12:15

By this it may be seen
who are the children of God,
and who are the children of the devil:
whoever does not do right is not of God,
nor he who does not love his brother.
I JOHN 3:10

What the Bible Says About...

Toil and Working

Thus says the Lord:
Keep your voice from weeping,
and your eyes from tears;
for your work shall be rewarded,
says the Lord.
JEREMIAH 31:36

For whatever a man sows,
that he will also reap.
GALATIANS 6:7

Do you see a man skillful in his work?
He will stand before kings;
he will not stand before obscure men.
PROVERBS 22:29

My chosen shall long enjoy
the work of their hands.
ISAIAH 65:22

Cursed is he who does the work
of the Lord with slackness.
JEREMIAH 48:10

But you take courage!
Do not let your hands be weak,
for your work shall be rewarded.
II CHRONICLES 15:7

Therefore,
do not be anxious about tomorrow,
for tomorrow will be anxious for itself.
let the day's own trouble
be sufficient for the day.
MATTHEW 6:34

Arise and be doing!
The Lord be with you!
I CHRONICLES 22:16

Let us run with perseverance
the race that is set before us,
looking to Jesus
the pioneer
and perfecter of our faith.
HEBREWS 12:1-2

Never flag in zeal, be aglow with the Spirit,
serve the Lord.
ROMANS 12:11

Do you not know that
in a race
all the runners compete,
but only one receives the prize?
So run that you may obtain it.
I CORINTHIANS 9:24

He who sows sparingly
will also reap sparingly,
and he who sows bountifully
will also reap bountifully.
II CORINTHIANS 9:6

Having gifts that differ
according to the grace given to us,
let us use them:
if prophecy, in proportion to our faith;
if service, in our serving;
he who teaches, in his teaching;
he who exhorts, in his exhortation;
he who contributes,
in liberality;
he who gives aid, with zeal;
he who does acts of mercy,
with cheerfulness.
ROMANS 12:6-8

If any one will not work, let him not eat.
II THESSALONIANS 3:10

Keep away from any brother
who is living in idleness.
II THESSALONIANS 3:6

And let us not grow weary in well-doing,
for in due season we shall reap, if we do not
lose heart.

GALATIANS 6:9

What the Bible Says About...

Problems and Suffering

Be strong, and of good courage.
Fear not;
be not dismayed;
for the Lord God is with you.
I CHRONICLES 28:20

Man that is born of a woman is of few days,
and full of trouble.
He comes forth like a flower,
and withers;
he flees like a shadow,
and continues not.
JOB 14:1-2

Blessed is the man
whom thou does chasten,
O Lord,
and whom thou dost teach
out of thy law
to give him respite from days of trouble,
until a pit is dug for the wicked.
PSALM 94:12-13

My son,
do not despise the Lord's discipline
or be weary of his reproof,
for the Lord reproves him whom he loves,
as a father
the son in whom he delights.
PROVERBS 3:11-12

And though the Lord give you
the head of adversity
and the water of affliction,
yet your teacher will not hide any more,
but your eyes shall see your teacher.
And your ears shall hear a word
behind you,
saying,
"This is the way, walk in it."
ISAIAH 30:20-21

Come, let us return to the Lord;
for he has torn,
that he may heal us;
he has stricken,
and he will bind us up.
HOSEA 6:1

Through many tribulations we must
enter the kingdom of God.
ACTS 14:22

If you faint in the day of adversity,
your strength is small.
PROVERBS 24:10

May those who sow in tears
reap with shouts of joy!
He that goes forth weeping,
bearing the seed for sowing,
shall come home with shouts of joy,
bringing his sheaves with him.
PSALM 126:5-6

Your sun shall no more go down, nor your
moon withdraw itself; for the Lord will be
your everlasting light, and your days of
mourning shall be ended.
ISAIAH 60:20

The Lord is good,
a stronghold in the day of trouble;
He knows those
who take refuge in Him.
NAHUM 1:7

I consider that
the sufferings of this present time
are not worth comparing
with the glory
that is to be revealed to us.
ROMANS 8:18

So we do not lose heart.
Though our outer nature is wasting away,
our inner nature
is being renewed every day.
For this slight momentary affliction
is preparing for us
an eternal weight of glory
beyond all comparison
because we look
not to the things that are unseen;
for the things that are seen are transient,
but the things that are unseen are eternal.
II CORINTHIANS 4:16-18

It was fitting that he,
for whom and by whom all things exist,
in bringing many sons to glory,
should make the pioneer of their salvation
perfect
through
suffering.
HEBREWS 2:10

My son,
do not regard lightly
the discipline of the Lord,
nor lose courage
when you are punished by Him.
For the Lord disciplines him
whom He loves,
and chastises every son
whom He receives.
HEBREWS 12:5-6

Blessed is the man who endures trial,
for when he has stood the test
he will receive the crown of life
which God has promised
to those who love him.
JAMES 1:12

Behold, I have refined you,
but not like silver;
I have tried you in the furnace of affliction.
ISAIAH 48:10

Weeping may tarry,
for the night,
but
joy comes with the morning.
PSALM 30:5

Because He Himself has suffered
and been tempted,
He is able to help
those who are tempted.
HEBREWS 2:18

What the Bible Says About...

Anger and Arguing

Drive out a scoffer,
and strife will go out,
and quarreling and abuse will cease.
PROVERBS 22:10

The beginning of strife
is like
letting out water;
so quit
before the quarrel breaks out.
PROVERBS 17:14

It is an honor for
a man
to keep aloof from strife;
but
every fool
will be quarreling.
PROVERBS 20:3

Better is a dry morsel with quiet
than a house full of feasting with strife.
PROVERBS 17:1

If possible,
so far as it depends on you,
live peaceably
with all.
ROMANS 12:18

Let all bitterness and wrath and anger
and clamor and slander
be put away from you,
with all malice
and be kind to one another,
tenderhearted,
forgiving one another,
as God in Christ forgave you.
EPHESIANS 4:31-32

As for a man who is factious,
after admonishing him
once or twice,
have nothing more to do with him.
TITUS 3:10

Let every man be quick to hear,
slow to speak,
slow to anger,
for the anger of man
does not work the righteousness of God.
JAMES 1:19

And the tongue is a fire.
The tongue is an unrighteous word
among our members,
staining the whole body,
setting on fire the cycle of nature,
and set on fire by hell.
For every kind of beast and bird,
of reptile and sea creature,
can be tamed and has been tamed
by humankind,
but no human being can tame the tongue.
With it
we bless the Lord and Father,
and with it
we curse men,
who are made in the likeness of God.
JAMES 3:6-12

Do not grumble,
brethren,
against one another,
that you may not be judged.
JAMES 5:9

He who meddles
in a quarrel not his own
is like one
who takes a passing dog by the ears.
PROVERBS 26:17

Make no friendship
with a man given to anger,
nor go with a wrathful man,
lest you learn his ways
and entangle yourself in a snare.
PROVERBS 22:24-25

What the Bible Says About...

Self-Reliance and Peace of Mind

In the thought of one who is at ease
there is contempt for misfortune.
JOB 12:5

Great peace have those
who love thy law;
nothing
can make them stumble.
PSALM 119:165

Better is a little
with the fear of the Lord
than great treasure and trouble with it.
Better is a dinner of herbs
where love is
than
a fatted ox and hatred with it.
PROVERBS 15:16-17

As you saw
the iron mixed with miry clay,
so
they will mix with one another in marriage,
but they will not hold together,
just as iron
does not mix with the clay.
DANIEL 2:43

Thou dost keep him in perfect peace,
whose mind is stayed on Thee,
because He trusts in thee.
Trust in the Lord for ever
for the Lord God is an everlasting rock.
ISAIAH 26:3-4

And the effect of righteousness will be
peace and the result of righteousness,
quietness and trust forever.
ISAIAH 32:17

But the wicked are like the tossing sea;
for it cannot rest,
and its waters toss up mire and dirt.
ISAIAH 57:20

A prophet is not without honor
except in his own country,
and among his own kin.
MARK 6:4

In the world you have tribulation;
but be of good cheer,
I have overcome the world.
JOHN 16:33

If the world hates you,
know that
it has hated me
before it hated you.
JOHN 15:18

We rejoice in our sufferings,
knowing that suffering produces endurance,
and endurance produces character,
and character produces hope,
and hope does not disappoint us,
because God's love
has been poured into our hearts
through the Holy Spirit
which has been given to us.
ROMANS 5:3-5

If you love me,
you will keep my commandments.
And I will pray the Father,
and He will give you another Counselor,
to be with you forever,
even the Spirit of truth,
whom the
world cannot receive,
because it neither sees him nor knows him;
you know him,
for he dwells with you, and will be in you.
JOHN 14:15-17

Do not be conformed to this world
but be transformed
by the renewal of your mind.
ROMANS 12:2

Rejoice
in your hope,
be patient
in tribulation,
be constant
in prayer.
ROMANS 12:12

As for the man who is weak in faith,
welcome him,
but not for disputes over opinions.
ROMANS 14:1

No temptation has overtaken you
that is not common to man.
God is faithful,
and He will not let you be
tempted beyond your strength,
but with the temptations
will also provide the way of escape,
that you may be able to endure it.
I CORINTHIANS 10:13

Live quietly,
mind your own affairs,
and work with your hands ...so that
you may command the respect of outsiders,
and be dependent on nobody.
I THESSALONIANS 4:11-12

There is no peace,
says the Lord,
for the wicked.
ISAIAH 48:22

They rest in their beds who walk
in their uprightness.
ISAIAH 57:2

Each man
will have to bear his own load.
GALATIANS 6:5

No prophet is acceptable
in his own country.
LUKE 4:24

Do not throw away your confidence,
which has a great reward.
For you have need of endurance,
so that you may do
the will of God
and receive what is promised.
HEBREWS 10:35-36

Be sober, be watchful.
Your adversary the devil
prowls around like a roaring lion,
seeking someone to devour.
Resist him, firm in your faith,
knowing that
the same experience of suffering
is required of your brotherhood
throughout the world.
I PETER 5:8

I have learned,
in whatever state I am,
to be content.
I know how to be abased,
and I know how to abound;
in any and all circumstances,
I have learned the secret of facing
plenty and hunger,
abundance and want.
I can do all things
in Him who strengthens me.
PHILIPPIANS 4:11-13

What the Bible Says About...

Justice and Wrongdoing

Justice,
and only justice,
you shall follow,
that you may live and inherit the land
which the Lord your God gives you.
DEUTERONOMY 16:20

You shall not have in your bag
two kinds of weights,
a large and a small.
You shall not have in your house
two kinds of measures,
a large and a small.
A full and just weight you shall have;
that your days may be prolonged
in the land which the Lord your God
gives you.
For all who do such things,
all who act dishonestly,
are an abomination to the Lord your God.
DEUTERONOMY 25:13-16

Better is a little with righteousness than
great revenues with injustice.
PROVERBS 16:8

Now, then,
let the fear of the Lord be upon you;
take heed what you do,
for there is no perversion of justice
with the Lord our God,
or partiality,
or taking bribes.
II CHRONICLES 19:7

When one rules justly over men,
ruling in the fear of God,
he dawns on them
like the morning light,
like the sun
shining forth upon a cloudless morning,
like rain
that makes grass to
sprout from the earth.
II SAMUEL 23:3-4

Woe to the wicked!
It shall be ill with him,
for what his hands have done
shall be done to him.
ISAIAH 3:11

Woe to those
who call evil good and good evil,
who put darkness for light
and light for darkness,
who put bitter for sweet
and sweet for bitter!
Woe to those
who are wise in their own eyes,
and shrewd in their own sight!
Woe to those
who are heroes at drinking wine,
and valiant men in mixing strong drink,
who acquit the guilty for a bribe,
and deprive the innocent of his right!
ISAIAH 5:20-23

There are six things
which the Lord hates,
seven which are an abomination to Him:
haughty eyes,
a lying tongue,
and hands that shed innocent blood,
a heart that devises wicked plans,
feet that make haste to run to evil,
a false witness who breathes out lies,
and a man who sows discord among brothers.
PROVERBS 6:16-19

Woe to the rebellious children, says the
Lord, who carry out a plan, but not mine;
and who make a league, but not of my
spirit, that they may add sin to sin.
ISAIAH 30:1

Behold,
the wicked man conceives evil,
and is pregnant with mischief,
and brings forth lies.
He makes a pit,
digging it out,
and falls into the hole which he has made.
His mischief
returns upon his own head,
and on
his own pate his violence descends.
PSALM 7:14-16

The dull man cannot know,
the stupid cannot understand this:
That, though the wicked sprout like grass
and all evildoers flourish,
they are doomed to destruction forever.
PSALM 92:6-7

There is no man who does not sin.
I KINGS 8:46

For the ruthless shall come to nought
and the scoffer cease,
and all who watch to do evil
shall be cut off.
ISAIAH 29:20

You should not have looted his goods
in the day of his calamity.
OBADIAH 13

Woe to him
who gets evil gain for his house,
to set his nest on high,
to be safe from the reach of harm!
You have devised shame
to your house
by cutting off many peoples,
you have forfeited your life.
HABAKKUK 2:9-10

For behold,
the day comes
burning like an oven,
when
all the arrogant
and all evildoers
will be stubble.
MALACHI 4:1

The iniquities of the wicked
ensnare him,
and he is caught in the toils of sin.
He dies for lack of discipline,
and because of his great folly
he is lost.
PROVERBS 5:22-23

They do not know how to do right,
says the Lord,
those who store up violence and robbery
in their strongholds.
AMOS 3:10

Woe to those who devise wickedness
and work evil upon their beds!
When the morning dawns,
they perform it,
because it is in the power of their hand.
They covet fields,
and seize them;
and houses,
and take them away;
they oppress a man and his house,
a man and his inheritance.
Therefore, thus says the Lord:
Behold, against this family
I am devising evil,
from which
you cannot remove your necks;
and you shall not walk haughtily,
for it will be an evil time.
MICAH 2:1-3

Love your enemies
and pray for those who persecute you,
so that
you may be sons
of your Father
who is in heaven.
MATTHEW 5:44-45

Love your enemies,
do good to those
who hate you,
bless those who curse you,
pray for those who abuse you ...
Be merciful,
even as your father is merciful.
LUKE 6:27-28...6:36

He who walks in integrity
walks securely,
but he who perverts his ways
will be found out.
PROVERBS 10:9

Bless those who persecute you; bless
and do not curse them.
ROMANS 12:14

Repay no one evil for evil,
but take thought for what is noble
in the sight of all.
ROMANS 12:17

Never avenge yourselves,
but leave it to the wrath of God;
for it is written,
"Vengeance is mine, I will repay,
says the Lord."
No,
if your enemy is hungry, feed him;
if he is thirsty, give him a drink;
for by so doing
you will heap burning coals upon his head.
Do not be overcome by evil,
but overcome evil with good.
ROMANS 12:19-21

Nothing is unclean in itself;
but it is unclean
for any one who thinks it is unclean.
If your brother is being injured
by what you eat,
you are no longer walking in love.
Do not let what you eat
cause the ruin
of one for whom Christ died.
ROMANS 14:14

It is not right to eat meat or drink wine
or do anything
that will make your brother stumble.
ROMANS 14:21

Now the works of the flesh are plain:
immorality,
impurity,
licentiousness,
idolatry,
sorcery,
enmity,
strife,
jealousy,
anger,
selfishness,
dissension,
party spirit,
envy,
drunkenness,
carousing,
and the like.
GALATIANS 5:19

Give no opportunity to the devil.
EPHESIANS 4:27

If we sin
deliberately
after receiving the knowledge of the truth,
there no longer
remains a sacrifice for sins,
but a fearful
prospect of judgement.
HEBREWS 10:26-27

Whoever knows what is right to do
and fails to do it,
for him it is sin.
JAMES 4:17

All wrongdoing is sin,
but there is sin
which is not mortal.
I JOHN 5:17

There is no peace,
says the Lord,
for the wicked.
ISAIAH 48:22

Do you not know this from of old,
since man was placed upon earth
that
the exulting
of the wicked is short,
and the joy of the godless
but for a moment?
JOB 20:4-5

What the Bible Says About...

Discipline and Self-Control

It is like sport to a fool
to do wrong,
but wise conduct is pleasure
to a man of understanding.
PROVERBS 10:23

Do not say,
I will do to him as he has done to me;
I will pay the man back for what he has
done.
PROVERBS 24:29

Answer not a fool according to his folly,
lest you be like him yourself.
PROVERBS 26:4

The righteous holds to his way,
and he that has clean hands
grows stronger and stronger.
JOB 17:9

The simple believes everything,
but the prudent looks where he is going.
A wise man is cautious
and turns away from evil,
but a fool throws off restraint
and is careless.
A man of quick temper
acts foolishly,
but a man of discretion
is patient.
PROVERBS 14:15-17

Surely vexation
kills the fool,
and jealousy
slays the simple.
JOB 5:2

Good sense makes a man
slow to anger,
and it is his glory
to overlook an offense.
PROVERBS 19:11

He who is slow to anger
has great understanding,
but he who has a hasty temper
exalts folly.
PROVERBS 14:29

A man without self-control
is like a city
broken into
and left without walls.
PROVERBS 25:28

A fool gives full vent to his anger,
but a wise man quietly holds it back.
PROVERBS 29:11

Be not quick to anger, for anger
lodges in the bosom of fools.
ECCLESIASTES 7:9

A soft answer turns away wrath,
but a harsh word stirs up anger.
PROVERBS 15:1

Has the Lord as great delight
in burnt offerings and sacrifices
as in obeying the voice of the Lord?
Behold,
to obey is better than sacrifice,
and to hearken than the fat of rams.
I SAMUEL 15:22

If one turns away from hearing the law,
even his prayer is an abomination.
PROVERBS 28:9

Has not the one God
made and sustained for us the spirit of life?
And what does he desire?
Godly offspring.
So take heed to yourselves,
and let none be faithless
to the wife of this youth,
for I hate divorce,
says the Lord the God of Israel,
and covering one's garment with violence,
says the Lord of Hosts.
So take heed to yourselves
and do not be faithless.
MALACHI 2:15-16

The friendship of the Lord
is for those who fear Him,
and He makes known to them
His covenant.
PSALM 25:14

Whoever loves discipline
loves knowledge,
but he who hates reproof
is stupid.
PROVERBS 12:1

All things are lawful for me, but not all
things are helpful. All things are lawful for
me, but I will not be enslaved by anything.
I CORINTHIANS 6:12

He who restrains his words has knowledge,
and he who has a cool spirit
is a man of understanding.
PROVERBS 17:27

Love is patient and kind;
love is not jealous or boastful;
it is not arrogant or rude.
Love does not insist on its own way;
it is not irritable or resentful;
it does not rejoice at wrong,
but rejoices in the right.
Love bears all things,
believes in all things,
hopes all things,
endures all things.
I CORINTHIANS 13:4-7

The vexation of a fool is known at once,
but the prudent man ignores an insult.
PROVERBS 12:16

What the Bible Says About...

Wealth and Power

You shall remember the Lord your God,
for it is He
who gives you power to get wealth.
DEUTERONOMY 8:11

Wealth brings many friends,
but a poor man
is deserted by his friends.
PROVERBS 19:4

Bread gained by deceit is sweet to a man,
but afterward
his mouth will be full of gravel.
PROVERBS 20:17

Like the partridge that gathers a brood
which she did not hatch,
so is he who gets riches
but not by right;
in the midst of his days
they will leave him,
and at his end he will be a fool.
JEREMIAH 17:11

Take heed,
and beware of all covetousness;
for a man's life
does not consist in
the abundance of his possessions.
LUKE 12:15

But those who desire to be rich
fall into temptations,
into a snare,
that plunge men into ruin and destruction.
For the love of money
is the root of all evils;
it is through this craving
that some have wandered away
from the faith
and pierced their hearts with many pangs.
I TIMOTHY 6:9-10

Keep your life free from
love of money,
and be content with what you have;
for He has said,
"I will never fail you nor forsake you."
HEBREWS 13:5

As for the rich in this world,
charge them not to be haughty,
nor to set their hopes on uncertain riches
but on God
who richly furnishes us
with everything to enjoy.
They are to do good,
to be rich in good deeds,
liberal and generous,
thus laying up for themselves
a good foundation for the future,
so that
they may take hold of the life
which is life indeed.

I TIMOTHY 6:17

What the Bible Says About...

Education, Knowledge, and Wisdom

A stupid man
will get understanding
when a wild ass's colt
is born a man.
JOB 11:12

"Knowledge" puffs up,
but love builds up.
I CORINTHIANS 8:1

If I speak
in the tongues of men and of angels,
but have not love,
I am a noisy gong or a clanging cymbal.
And if I have prophetic powers,
and understand all mysteries
and all knowledge,
and if I have all faith,
so as to remove mountains,
but have not love, I am nothing.
I CORINTHIANS 13:1-2

Love never ends;
as for prophecies, they will pass away;
as for tongues, they will cease;
as for knowledge, it will pass away.
For our knowledge is imperfect
and our prophecy is imperfect,
but when the perfect comes,
the imperfect will pass away.
I CORINTHIANS 13:8-10

The love of Christ ... surpasses knowledge.
EPHESIANS 3:19

See to it
that no one makes a prey of you
by philosophy
and empty deceit,
according to human tradition,
according to the
elemental spirits of the universe,
and not according to Christ.
COLOSSIANS 2:8

Look carefully how you walk,
not as unwise then
but as wise,
making the most of your times,
because the days are evil.
Therefore
do not be foolish
but understand
what the will of the Lord is.
EPHESIANS 5:15-17

Avoid the godless chatter
and contradictions
of what is falsely called knowledge,
for by professing it
some have missed the mark
as regards
the faith.
I TIMOTHY 6:20-21

Do not be led away
by diverse and
strange teachings.
HEBREWS 13:9

There are many
insubordinate men,
empty talkers
and deceivers ...
since they are upsetting whole families
by teaching for base gains
what they have no right to teach.
TITUS 1:10-11

Avoid stupid controversies,
genealogies,
dissensions
and quarrels over the law,
for they are unprofitable and futile.
TITUS 3:9

Who is wise and understanding
among you?
By his good life
let him show his works
in the
meekness of wisdom.
JAMES 3:13

But the wisdom from above
is
first pure,
then peaceable,
gentle,
open to reason,
full of mercy and good fruits,
without uncertainty
or insincerity.
JAMES 3:17

Happy is
the man who finds wisdom,
and the man who gets understanding,
for the gain from it
is better
than gain from silver
and its profit
better than gold.
PROVERBS 3:13-14

Knowledge puffs up,
but love builds up.
I CORINTHIANS 8:1

And God said to man:
"Behold the fear of the Lord,
that is wisdom;
And
to depart from evil
is understanding."
JOB 28:28

Be not wise in your own eyes;
fear the Lord,
and turn away from evil.
It will be healing to your flesh,
and refreshment to your bones.
PROVERBS 3:7-8

Do you see a man
who is wise in his own eyes?
There is more hope for a fool
than for him.
PROVERBS 26:12

The Lord God has given me
the tongue of those who are taught,
that I may know
how to sustain with a word him that is
weary.
ISAIAH 50:4

But it is the spirit in a man,
the breath of the Almighty,
that makes him understand.
It is not the old
that are wise,
nor the aged
that understand
what is right.
JOB 32:8-9

A fool
takes no pleasure in understanding,
but only in
expressing an opinion.
PROVERBS 18:2

What the Bible Says About...

Honesty, Pride, and Honor

Thus says the Lord:
Let not the wise man
glory in this wisdom,
let not the mighty man
glory in his might;
let not the rich man
glory in his riches;
but let him who glories glory in this,
that he understands me,
that I am the Lord
who practices steadfast love,
justice,
and righteousness in the earth;
for in these things
I delight says the Lord.
JEREMIAH 9:23-24

For though the Lord is high,
he regards the lowly;
but the haughty he knows from afar.
PSALM 138:6

How forceful are honest words!
JOB 6:25

The haughty looks of man
shall be brought low,
and the pride of men
shall be humbled;
and the Lord alone
will be exalted in that day.
For the Lord of Hosts
has a day
against all that is proud and lofty,
against all that is lifted up and high.
ISAIAH 2:11-12

The proud
one day
shall stumble and fall,
with none to raise him up.
JEREMIAH 50:32

He who ignores instruction
despises himself,
but he who heeds admonition
gains understanding.
The fear of the Lord is
instruction in wisdom,
and humility goes before honor.
PROVERBS 15:32-33

Pride goes
before destruction,
and a haughty spirit
before a fall.

PROVERBS 16:18

Before destruction
a man's heart is haughty,
but humility
goes before honor.

PROVERBS 18:12

Beware of
practicing your piety before men
in order to be seen by them,
for then
you will have no reward
from your Father
who is in heaven.

MATTHEW 6:1

Let him who boasts,
boast of the Lord.
For it is not the man
who commends himself
that is accepted,
but the man whom the Lord commends.
II CORINTHIANS. 10:17-18

Outdo one another
in showing honor.
ROMANS 12:10

What the Bible Says About...

Gifts and Giving

Each one must do
as he has made up his mind,
not reluctantly
or under compulsion,
for
God loves a cheerful giver.
II CORINTHIANS 9:7

Every man shall give
as he is able
according to
the blessing of the Lord your God
which He has given you.
DEUTERONOMY 16:17

You bring
what has been taken by violence
or is lame or sick,
and this you bring as your offering!
Shall I accept this from your hand?
Says the Lord.
Cursed be the cheat
who has a male in his flock, and vows it,
and yet sacrifices to the Lord
what is blemished.
MALACHI 1:13-14

When you make a vow
to the Lord your God,
you shall not be slack to pay it;
for the Lord your God
will surely require it of you,
and it would be sin in you...
You shall be careful to perform
what has passed your lips,
for you have voluntarily vowed
to the Lord your God
what you have promised
with your mouth.
DEUTERONOMY 23:21-23

I will pay
my vows to the Lord
in the presence
of all his people.
PSALM 116:14

It is more blessed
to give
than to receive.
ACTS 20:35

Bring the full tithes
into the storehouse,
that there may be food in my house;
and thereby
put me to the test,
says the Lord of Hosts,
if I will not
open the windows of heaven for you
and pour down for you
an overflowing blessing.
I will rebuke the devourer for you,
so that
it will not destroy the fruits of your soil;
and your vine in the field
shall not fail to bear,
says the Lord of Hosts.
Then all nations will call you blessed,
for you will be a land of delight,
says the Lord of Hosts.
MALACHI 3:10-12

If I give away all I have,
and if I deliver my body to be burned,
but have not love,
I gain nothing.
I CORINTHIANS 13:3

Do not neglect
to show hospitality to strangers,
for thereby
some have entertained angels
unaware.
HEBREWS 13:2

What the Bible Says About...

Children, Husbands, and Wives

Lo,
sons are a heritage from the Lord,
the fruit of the womb
a reward.
PSALM 127:3

Discipline your son
while there is hope;
do not
set your heart
on his destruction.
PROVERBS 19:18

Train up a child
in the way he should go
and when he is old
he will not depart from it.
PROVERBS 22:6

Folly is bound up
in the heart of a child,
but the rod of discipline
drives it far from him.
PROVERBS 22:15

Do not
withhold discipline from a child;
if you beat him with a rod,
he will not die.
If you beat him with the rod
you will save his life from hell.
PROVERBS 23:13-14

The rod and reproof give wisdom,
but
a child left to himself
brings shame to his mother.
PROVERBS 29:15

Discipline your son,
and he will give you rest;
he will give delight to your heart.
PROVERBS 29:17

Like a gold ring
in a swine's snout
is
a beautiful woman
without discretion.
PROVERBS 11:22

101

For the lips of a loose woman
drip honey,
and her speech
is smoother than oil;
but
in the end
she is
bitter as wormwood,
sharp as a two-edged sword.
PROVERBS 5:3-4

For children ought not
to lay up for
their parents,
but parents for their children.
II CORINTHIANS 12:14

He who loves his wife
loves himself.
EPHESIANS 5:28

A good wife
who can find?
She is far more precious than jewels,
The heart of her husband trusts in her,
And he will have no lack of gains.
She does him good, and not harm,
all the days of her life.
She seeks wool and flax, and
works with willing hands.
She is like the ships of the merchants,
She brings her food from afar.
She rises while it is yet night
and provides food for her household
and tasks for her maidens.
She considers a field and buys it;
with the fruit of her hands
she plants a vineyard.
Strength and dignity are her clothing,
And she laughs at the time to come,
She opens her mouth with wisdom,
And the teaching of kindness
is on her tongue.
She looks well
to the ways of her household,
And does not eat the bread of idleness.
Charm is deceitful, and beauty is vain,
But a woman who fears the Lord
is to be praised.
Give her of the fruit of her hands,
And let her works praise her in the gates.
PROVERBS 31:10-31

What is your life?
For you are a mist
that appears
for a little time
and then vanishes.
JAMES 4:14

Husbands,
love your wives,
and
do not be harsh with them.
COLOSSIANS 3:19

What the Bible Says About...

Family, Friends, and Neighbors

Do not eat the bread
of a man who is stingy;
do not desire his delicacies;
for he is like one
who is inwardly reckoning,
"Eat and drink!" he says to you;
but his heart is not with you.
PROVERBS 23:6-7

Let your foot
be seldom in your neighbor's house,
lest
he become weary of you
and hate you.
PROVERBS 25:17

... agree with one another,
live in peace,
and
the God of love and peace
will be with you.
II CORINTHIANS 13:11

But
you should not have gloated
over the day of your brother
in the day of his misfortune.
OBADIAH 12

But I say to you that
every one who is angry with his brother
shall be liable to judgement;
whoever insults his brother
shall be liable to the council;
and whoever says, "you fool!"
shall be liable to the hell of fire.
So if you are offering your gift at the altar
and there remember that
your brother has something against you,
leave your gift there
before the altar
and go
first to be reconciled to your brother,
then offer your gifts.
MATTHEW 5:22-24

If I,
your Lord and Teacher,
have washed your feet,
you also ought to wash one another's feet.
For
I have given you an example,
that
you should also do as I have done to you.
JOHN 13:14-15

A new commandment I give to you
that
you love one another;
even as I have loved you,
that you also love one another.
By this
all men will know that
you are my disciples,
if you have love for one another.
JOHN 13:34-35

Owe no one anything,
except
to love one another.
ROMANS 13:8

This is my commandment,
that you love one another
as I have loved you.
Greater love has no man
for his friends
than this,
that a man
lay down his life.
JOHN 15:12-13

Love one another
with brotherly affection.
ROMANS 12:10

Contribute to the need of the saints;
practice hospitality.
ROMANS 12:13

He
who withholds kindness from a friend
forsakes
the fear of the Almighty.
JOB 6:14

The commandments ..
are summed up in this sentence,
"You shall love your neighbor as yourself."
Love does no wrong to a neighbor;
therefore
love is the fulfilling of the law.
ROMANS 13:9-10

What the Bible Says About...

Sin and Repenting

Remember not the former things,
nor consider the things of old,
Behold,
I am doing a new thing:
now it springs forth,
do you not perceive it?

ISAIAH 43:18-19

For you
if you truly amend your ways
and your doings,
if you truly execute justice
with one another,
if you do not oppress the alien,
the fatherless or the widow,
or shed innocent blood in this place,
and if you do not go after other gods
to your own hurt,
then I will let you dwell in this place,
in the land that I gave of old
to your fathers
forever.

JEREMIAH 7:5-7

Yet even now,
says the Lord,
return to me with all your heart,
with fasting,
with weeping,
and with mourning;
and rend your hearts
and not your garments.
Return to the Lord, your God,
for
he is gracious and merciful,
slow to anger,
abounding in steadfast love,
and repents of evil.
JOEL 2:12-13

Thus says the Lord of Hosts:
consider how you have fared ...
you have looked for much,
and lo,
it came to little;
and when you brought it home,
I blew it away.
Why?
Says the Lord of Hosts,
because of my house that lies in ruins,
while you busy yourselves
each with his own house.
HAGGAI 1:7-9

If your hand
or your foot
causes you to sin,
cut it off
and throw it from you.
MATTHEW 18:8

It is better
to take refuge in the Lord
than
to put confidence in man.
PSALM 118:8

The fear of the Lord
is the beginning of knowledge;
fools
despise wisdom and instruction.
PROVERBS 1:7

The fear of the Lord
is hatred of evil.
PROVERBS 8:13

Thus says the Lord:
Cursed is the man who trusts in man
and makes flesh his aim,
whose heart turns away from the Lord.
He is like a shrub in the desert,
and shall not see any good come.
JEREMIAH 17:5-6

What profit is an idol
when its maker has shaped it,
a metal image,
a teacher of lies?
For the workman trusts
in his own creation
when he makes dumb idols!
HABAKKUK 2:18

Leave the presence of a fool,
for there
you do not meet
words of knowledge.
PROVERBS 14:7

And the Lord said:
Because this people
draw near with their mouth
and honor me with their lips,
while their hearts are far from me,
and their fear of me
is a commandment of new learned by rote;
therefore, behold,
I will again do marvelous things
with this people,
wonderful and marvelous,
and the wisdom of their wise men
shall perish,
and the discernment
of their discerning men shall be led.
ISAIAH 29:13-14

He who conceals his transgressions
will not prosper,
but he who confesses
and forsakes
them
will obtain mercy.
PROVERBS 28:13

Bear fruit
that befits repentance.
MATTHEW 3:10

Turn now
every one of you
from his evil way,
and amend your doings,
and do not go after other gods
to serve them,
and then
you shall dwell in the land
which I gave
to you and your fathers.
JEREMIAH 35:15

For
if you forgive men their trespasses,
your Heavenly Father also will forgive you;
but
if you do not forgive men their trespasses,
neither will your Father
forgive your trespasses.
MATTHEW 6:14-15

You shall not
fear other gods
or bow yourselves to them
or serve them
or sacrifice to them;
but you shall fear the Lord;
you shall bow yourselves to Him,
and
to Him you shall sacrifice.
II KINGS 17:35-36

As for me,
I would seek God,
and to God
would I commit my cause;
who does great things and unsearchable,
marvelous things without number:
he gives rain upon the earth
and sends water upon the fields;
he sets on high
those who are lowly,
and those who mourn
are lifted to safety.
JOB 5:8-11

Let
the words of my mouth
and the meditation of my heart
be acceptable in thy sight,
O Lord,
my rock and my redeemer.
PSALM 19:14

The sacrifice acceptable to God
is a broken spirit:
a broken and contrite heart,
O God,
thou wilt not despise.
PSALM 51:17

Is not this the fast that I choose:
to loose the hands of wickedness,
to undo the thongs of the yoke,
to let the oppressed go free,
and
to break every yoke?
ISAIAH 58:6

Those who pay regard
to vain idols
forsake their true loyalty.
JONAH 2:8

I hate, I despise your feasts,
and I take no delight
in your solemn assemblies.
AMOS 5:21

Unless a grain of wheat
falls into the earth
and dies,
it remains alone;
but if it dies,
it bears much fruit.
He who loves his life loses it,
and he who hates his life in this world
will keep it for eternal life.
If any one serves me,
he must follow me.
JOHN 12:24-26

The fruit of the Spirit is
love,
joy,
peace,
patience,
kindness,
goodness,
faithfulness,
gentleness,
self-control.
GALATIANS 5:22

Put off your old nature
which belongs to
your former manner of life,
and is corrupt through deceitful lusts,
and be renewed in the spirit of your minds,
and put on the new nature,
created after the likeness of God
in true righteousness
and holiness.
EPHESIANS 4:22-24

Work out your own salvation
with fear and trembling:
for God is at work in you,
both to will
and to work
for his good pleasure.
PHILIPPIANS 2:12-13

Draw near to God
and
he will draw near to you.
JAMES 4:8

For it would have been better for them
never to have known
the way of righteousness
than
after knowing it
to turn back from the holy commandment
delivered to men.
It has happened to them
according to the true proverb,
the dog turns back to his own vomit
and the sow is washed
only to wallow in the mire.
II PETER 2:21-22

If we say we have no sin,
we deceive ourselves,
and the truth is not in us.
If we confess our sins,
he is faithful and just,
and will forgive our sins
and cleanse us
from all unrighteousness.
I JOHN 1:8-9

He who says
he is in the light
and hates his brother
is in the darkness
still.
I JOHN 2:9

He
who does not love
remains
in death.
I JOHN 3:14

Those whom I love,
I reprove and chasten;
so
be zealous and repent.
REVELATION 3:19

Arise and go,
for this is no place to rest;
because of uncleanness
that destroys
with a grievous destruction.
MICAH 2:10

What the Bible Says About...

Judgement and Mercy

The fathers
shall not be put to death
for the children,
nor shall the children
be put to death
for the fathers;
every man shall be put to death
for his own sin.
DEUTERONOMY 24:16

For a tree is
known by its fruits.
MATTHEW 12:33

As you have done,
it shall be done to you;
your deeds
shall return on your own head.
OBADIAH 1:15

Do not judge by appearances
but judge
with right judgement.
JOHN 7:24

God has shown me
that
I should not call any man
common or unclean.
ACTS 10:28

Truly I perceive
that God shows no partiality
but in every nation
one who fears him
and does what is right
is acceptable to him.
ACTS 10:34

He who
through faith
is righteous
shall live.
GALATIANS 3:11

For in the resurrection
they neither marry
nor are given in marriage,
but are like angels in heaven.
MATTHEW 22:30

He who walks righteously
and speaks uprightly,
who despises the gain of oppression,
who shakes his hand,
lest they hold a bribe,
who stops his ears
from hearing of bloodshed,
and shuts his eyes
from looking upon evil,
he will dwell on the heights;
his place of defense will be
the fortress of rocks;
his bread will be given him,
his water
will be sure.

ISAIAH 33:15-16

Cursed be
he who perverts
the justice due
to the sojourners,
the fatherless,
and the widow.

DEUTERONOMY 27:19

For the Lord sees
not as man sees:
man looks on the outward appearance,
but
the Lord
looks on the heart.
I SAMUEL 16:7

Do not envy
a man of violence
and do not choose any of his ways;
for the perverse man
is an abomination to the Lord,
but the upright are in his confidence.
The Lord's curse is
on the house of the wicked,
but he blesses
the abode of the righteous.
PROVERBS 3:31-33

He who pursues
righteousness and kindness
will find
life and honor.
PROVERBS 21:21

The reward for humility
and fear of the Lord
is
riches and honor and life.
PROVERBS 22:4

Fret not yourself
because of evildoers,
and be not envious of the wicked;
for the evil man
has no future;
the lamp of the wicked will be put out.
PROVERBS 24:19-20

The dust returns to the earth
as it was,
and the
spirit returns
to God
who gave it.
ECCLESIASTES 12:7

Fear God,
and keep his commandments;
for this is the whole duty of man.
For God will bring every deed
into judgement
with every secret thing,
whether good or evil.
ECCLESIATES 12:13-14

Woe to the wicked!
It shall be ill with him
for
what his hands have done
shall be done to him.
ISAIAH 3:11

According to their deeds,
so will he repay,
wrath
to his adversaries,
requital
to his enemies.
ISAIAH 59:18

Now therefore
hear this,
you lover of pleasures,
who sit securely,
who say in your heart,
"I am and there is no one besides one;
I shall not sit as a widow
or know the loss of children:"
These two things shall come to you
in a moment in one day;
the loss of children
and widowhood
shall come upon you in full measure,
in spite of your many sorceries
and the great power of your enchantments.
ISAIAH 47:8-9

But every one shall die for his own sin;
each man who eats sour grapes,
his teeth shall be set on edge.
JEREMIAH 31:30

Therefore I will judge you,
O house of Israel,
every one according to his ways,
says the Lord God.
EZEKIEL 18:30

Behold,
I will requite your deeds
upon
your head,
says the Lord God.
EZEKIEL 16:43

But you who forsake the Lord,
who forget my holy mountains,
who set a table for fortune
and fill cups of mixed wine for destiny;
I will destine you to the sword, and
all of you shall bow down to the slaughter;
because,
when I called,
you did not answer,
when I spoke,
you did not listen,
but did what was evil in my eyes,
and chose
what I did not delight in.
ISAIAH 65:11-12

And many of those
who sleep in the dust of the earth
shall awake,
some to everlasting life,
and some
to shame and everlasting contempt
and those who are wise
shall shine
like the brightness of the firmament,
and those who turn many to righteousness
like the stars for ever and ever.
DANIEL 12:2-3

For the day of the Lord is coming,
it is near,
a day of darkness and gloom,
a day
of clouds
and rich darkness.
JOEL 2:1-2

As you have done,
it shall be done to you,
your deeds shall return on your own head.
OBADIAH 15

And on that day,
says the Lord God,
"I will make the sun go down at noon,
and darken the earth in mourning,
I will turn your feasts into mourning,
and all your songs into lamentation;
I will bring sackcloth upon all loins,
and baldness on every head;
I will make it
like the mourning for an only son,
and the end of it
like a bitter day."
AMOS 8:9-10

Woe to my worthless shepherd,
who deserts the flock!
May the sword smite
his arm and his right eye!
Let his arm be wholly withered,
his right eye utterly blinded.
ZECHARIAH 11:17

Neither their silver
nor their gold
shall be able to deliver them
on the day of
the wrath of the Lord.
ZEPHANIAH 1:18

For the Lord God of hosts
has
a day of tumult
and trampling
and confusion
in the valley of vision,
a battering down of walls
and
a shouting to the mountains.
ISAIAH 22:5

The soul that sins shall die.
The son shall not suffer
for the iniquity of the father,
nor the father suffer
for the iniquity of the son;
the righteousness of the righteous
shall be upon himself,
and the wickedness of the wicked
shall be upon himself.
EZEKIEL 18:20

Thus
you will know them
by their fruits.
MATTHEW 7:20

Judge not,
that you not be judged.
For with the judgement you pronounce
you will be judged,
and the measure you give
will be the measure you get.
MATTHEW 7:1-2

Enter by the narrow gate;
for the gate is wide and the way is easy,
that leads to destruction,
and those who enter by it are many. For the
gate is narrow and the way is hard, that
leads to life,
and those who find it are few.
MATTHEW 7:13-14

Those who are well
have no need of a physician,
but those who are sick
go and learn what this means,
'I desire mercy, and not sacrifice.'
For I came
not to call the righteous,
but sinners.
MATTHEW 9:12-13

And this is eternal life,
that they know
Thee
the only true God,
and
Jesus Christ
whom Thou has sent.
JOHN 17:3

Therefore
you have no excuse,
O man,
whoever you are,
when you judge another;
for in passing judgement upon him
you condemn yourself,
because you,
the judge,
are doing the very same things.
ROMANS 2:1

If you confess with your lips
that Jesus is Lord
and believe in your heart
that God raised him from the dead,
you will be saved.
ROMANS 10:9

Let not him who eats
despise
him who abstains,
and let not him who abstains
pass judgement
on him who eats,
for God has welcomed him.
Who are you
to pass judgement
on the servant of another?
ROMANS 14:3

For
we must all appear
before the judgement seat of Christ,
so that
each one may receive good or evil,
according to what he has done in the body.
II CORINTHIANS 5:10

Their end
will correspond
to their deeds.
II CORINTHIANS 11:15

The day of the Lord
will come
like
a thief in the night.
I THESSALONIANS 5:2

For judgement is
without mercy
to one
who has shown no mercy;
yet mercy
triumphs over judgement.
JAMES 2:13

A man
is justified by works
and not by faith alone.
JAMES 2:24

If any one
slays with the sword,
with the sword
he must be slain.
REVELATIONS 13:10

What the Bible Says About...

Faith and Religion

And Jesus answered them:
Truly I say to you,
if you have faith and never doubt,
you will not only do
what has been done to the fig tree,
but even if you say to this mountain,
'Be taken up and cast into the sea,'
it will be done.
And whatever you ask in prayer,
you will receive if you have faith.
MATTHEW 21: 21

Behold,
he whose soul is not upright in him
shall fall,
but the righteous
shall live by his faith.
HABAKKUK 2:4

He who believes
will not be
in haste.
ISAIAH 28:16

Though the fig tree do not blossom,
nor fruit be on the vines,
the produce of the olive fail and the fields
yield no food,
the flock be cut off from the fold,
and there be no herd in the stalls,
yet I will rejoice in the Lord,
I will joy in the God of my salvation.
God, the Lord, is my strength,
He makes my feet like hinds' feet,
He makes me tread upon my high places.
HABAKKUK 3:17-19

For every one who asks
receives,
and he who seeks
finds,
and to him who knocks
it will be opened.
MATTHEW 7:8

So everyone who acknowledges me
before men,
I also will acknowledge
before my Father
who is in heaven.
MATTHEW 10:32

He who
through faith
is righteous
shall live.
ROMANS 1:17

Faith is
the assurance of things
hoped for,
the conviction of things
not seen.
HEBREWS 11:1

By faith we understand
that the world was created
by the word of God,
so that
what is seen
was
made out of things
which do not appear.
HEBREWS 11:3

Have no anxiety about anything,
but in everything
by prayer and supplication
with thanksgiving
let your request be known to God.
PHILIPPIANS 4:6

If any thinks he is religious,
and does not bridle his tongue
but deceives his heart,
this man's religion is vain.
Religion that is pure and undefiled
before God and the Father
is this:
to visit orphans and widows
in their affliction,
and to keep oneself unstained
from the world.
JAMES 1:26-27

Faith by itself,
if it has no works,
is dead.
JAMES 2:17

Faith
apart from the works
is dead.
JAMES 2:26

Unfaithful creatures!
Do you not know
that
friendship with the world
makes himself
an enemy of God.
JAMES 4:4

If any among you
wanders from the truth
and some one brings him back,
let him know that
whoever brings back a sinner
from the error of his way
will save his soul
from death
and
will cover a multitude of sins.
JAMES 5:20

Let not many of you become
teachers,
for you know that
we who teach
shall
be judged
with greater strictness.
JAMES 3:1

Baptism
now saves you,
not as a removal of dirt from the body but
as an appeal to God
for a clear conscience.
I PETER 3:21

Make every effort
to supplement your faith
with virtue,
and virtue with knowledge,
and knowledge with self-control
and self-control with steadfastness,
and steadfastness with godliness,
and godliness with brotherly affection,
and brotherly affection with love.
II PETER 1:5-7

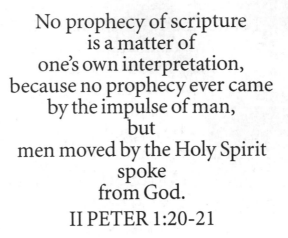

No prophecy of scripture
is a matter of
one's own interpretation,
because no prophecy ever came
by the impulse of man,
but
men moved by the Holy Spirit
spoke
from God.
II PETER 1:20-21

Be
doers of the word,
and not
hearers only.
JAMES 1:22

What the Bible Says About...

God

The Lord is the everlasting God,
the creator of the ends of the earth.
He does not faint or grow weary,
his understanding is unsearchable.
He gives power to the faint,
and to him who has no might
he increases strength.
Even youths shall faint and be weary,
and young men shall fall exhausted;
but
they who wait for the Lord
shall renew their strength,
they shall mount up with wings like eagles,
they shall run and not be weary,
they shall walk and not faint.
ISAIAH 40:28-31

Fear not,
for I am with you,
be not dismayed,
for I am your God;
I will strengthen you,
I will help you,
I will uphold you
with
my victorious right hand.
ISAIAH 41:10

O great and mighty…is the Lord of Hosts,
great in counsel
and mighty in deed;
whose eyes are open to all the ways of men,
rewarding every man according to his ways
and according to the fruit of his doings.
JEREMIAH 32:18-19

The steadfast love of the Lord
never ceases,
His mercies
never come to an end;
they are new every morning,
great is Thy faithfulness.
The Lord is my portion,
says my soul,
therefore, I will hope in Him.
The Lord is good
to those who wait for him,
to the soul that seeks Him.
LAMENTATIONS 3:22-25

But
the Lord is a refuge to his people,
a stronghold to the people of Israel.
JOEL 3:16

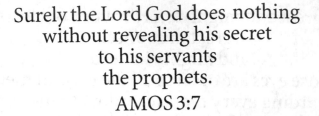

Surely the Lord God does nothing
without revealing his secret
to his servants
the prophets.
AMOS 3:7

The Lord is my rock,
my fortress,
and my deliverer,
my god,
my rock,
in whom I take refuge,
my shield and the horn of my salvation,
my stronghold and my refuge,
my savior;
thou savest me from violence.
I call upon the Lord,
who is worthy to be praised,
and I am saved from my enemies.
II SAMUEL 22:1-4

Thou art a gracious God
and merciful, slow to anger,
and abounding in steadfast love,
and repentest of evil.
JONAH 4:2

As you do not know
how the spirit comes to the bones
in
the womb of a woman with child,
so you do not know
the work of God
who makes everything.
ECCLESIASTES 11:5

God sent forth his Son,
born of woman.
Born under the law,
to redeem those who were under the law,
so that we might receive
adoption
as sons.
GALATIANS 4:4-5

For by grace
you have been saved
through faith;
and this is not your own doing,
it is the gift of God.
EPHESIANS 2:8

Therefore
let us be grateful
for receiving a kingdom
that cannot be shaken,
and thus
let us offer to God
acceptable worship,
with reverence and awe;
for God is a consuming fire.
HEBREWS 12:28-29

But do not ignore this one fact,
that
with the Lord
one day is
as a thousand years,
and a thousand years
as one day.
II PETER 3:8

I am coming soon,
bringing my recompense,
to repay every one
for what he has done.
REVELATION 22:12

Let us love one another;
for love is of God,
and he who loves
is born of God and knows God.
He who does not love
does not know God;
for God is love.
1 JOHN 4:7-8

I am the Alpha and the Omega,
the beginning and the end.
To the thirsty I will give water
without price
from
the fountain of the water of life.
REVELATION 21:6

What the Bible Says About...

Love

You shall love the Lord your God
with all your heart,
and with all your soul,
and with all your mind.
This is the great and first commandment.
And a second is like it:
you shall love your neighbor as yourself.
On these two commandments
depend
all the law and the prophets.
MATTHEW 22:37

Let love be genuine;
hate what is evil;
hold fast to what is good.
ROMANS 12:9

The love of Christ ...
surpasses knowledge.
EPHESIANS 3:18

Knowledge puffs up,
but love builds up.
I CORINTHIANS 8:1

He who loves his wife
loves himself.
EPHESIANS 5:28

Husbands,
love your wives,
and
do not be harsh with them.
COLOSSIANS 3:19

If I speak
in the tongues of men and of angels,
but have not love,
I am a noisy gong or a clanging cymbal.
And
though I have prophetic powers, and
understand all mysteries and all knowledge,
and if I have all faith,
so as to remove mountains,
but have not love,
I am nothing.
And though
I bestow all my goods to feed the poor
and even give my own body to be burned,
if I have not love,
I gain nothing.
Love suffers all things, and is kind.
Love does not envy.
Love is not puffed up.
Love does not behave selfishly,
seeking one's own way,
nor is love easily provoked.
Love does not think evil.
Love does not rejoice in wrong doing,
but rejoices in the truth.
Love bears all things,
believes all things,
hopes all things,
endures all things.

Love never fails.
As for prophecies,
they will fail.
As for tongues, they will cease.
Knowledge also will vanish.
For our knowledge is imperfect
and our prophecies are also imperfect …
And now
center your life on
faith,
hope,
and love,
these three.
But the greatest of these is love.
I CORINTHIANS 13:1-13

This is my commandment, that you
love one another as I have loved you.
Greater love has no man for his friends
than this,
that a man lay down his life.
JOHN 15:12-13

Love never ends;
as for prophecies, they will pass away;
as for tongues, they will cease;
as for knowledge, it will pass away.
For our knowledge is imperfect
and our prophecy is imperfect,
but when the perfect comes,
the imperfect will pass away.
I CORINTHIANS 13:8-10

Owe no one anything,
except
to love one another.
ROMANS 13:8

Love one another
with brotherly affection.
ROMANS 12:10

A new commandment I give to you
that
you love one another;
even as I have loved you,
that you also love one another.
By this all men will know that
you are my disciples,
if you have love
for one another.
JOHN 13:34-35

The commandments ..
are summed up in this sentence,
"You shall love your neighbor as yourself."
Love does no wrong to a neighbor;
therefore love is the fulfilling of the law
ROMANS 13:9

Love is patient and kind;
love is not jealous or boastful;
it is not arrogant or rude.
Love does not insist on its own way;
it is not irritable or resentful;
it does not rejoice at wrong,
but rejoices in the right.
Love bears all things,
believes in all things,
hopes all things,
endures all things.

I CORINTHIANS 13:4-7

Love your enemies,
do good to those who hate you,
bless those who curse you,
pray for those who abuse you …
be merciful,
even as your father is merciful.

LUKE 6:27

Let us love one another;
for love is of God,
and he who loves
is born of God and knows God.
He who does not love
does not know God;
for God is love.

I JOHN 4:7-8

About the Author

Patty Sleem holds an MBA from the Harvard Business School and a BA in English from the University of North Carolina at Chapel Hill. A noted public speaker, writer, and teacher, she is the author of *Back In Time* and *Second Time Around*. She can be reached through e-mail at preppub@aol.com.

READER'S GUIDE FOR

What the Bible Says About...

Patty Sleem

PREP Publishing
Fayetteville, North Carolina

Talking Things Over with Patty Sleem

Q: What led you to write this book?

Patty Sleem: I am fascinated with the Bible, and I'm convinced that this "good book" has the ability to provide wise advice that will help us live our lives in a meaningful way.

Q: When did you get your start as an author?

Patty Sleem: I began writing when I was a youth, and after majoring in English at the University of North Carolina at Chapel Hill, I gravitated toward jobs in writing, public relations, journalism, and communications. For the past 20 years I have worked for a publisher, and I play a key role in selecting and editing the religion titles published by PREP Publishing.

Q: We hear a lot about "inspiration." Is that a factor in your work?

Patty Sleem: Inspiration is what makes a writer persist in completing a book, even when the pressure of work and life events make it difficult to find time.

Q: How did you figure out what sections you wanted in the book?

Patty Sleem: I tried to find common themes that would have relevance for nearly everyone. For example, "Self-Reliance and Peace of Mind" is a subject which is meaningful to anyone, so I wanted to compile passages from the Bible on that subject which I thought would help people find direction in that area of their lives. Similarly, I thought it would be interesting to see what the Bible says about "Children, Husbands, and Wives" so I developed that section.

Q: When do you write? Do you have a particular schedule you follow? And do you write using a computer or using pen and paper?

Patty Sleem: I write using a computer now, and I've found that the rewriting and revisions are much easier using a computer. I don't feel that I've given up anything by not having the "feel" of the pen and paper. In terms of my writing schedule, I usually have deadlines by which I must get a book to my publisher, so I often find time on the weekend to do most of the work in my home office.

169

Q: Is all of your writing pretty much Bible oriented?

Patty Sleem: No. I have a "day job" as an editor for a publishing company and, in that job, I am involved in editing how-to books on jobs and careers. I also help my publisher identify new religion books for future publication.

Q: What do you do when you're not writing?

Patty Sleem: In addition to my full-time job, I'm a wife and mother. We have four children. When my children were younger, I was extensively involved in Cub Scouting and Boy Scouting while my three boys (as well as my daughter) were involved in Scouting. I have been an adult Sunday School teacher as well as a teacher for children's classes. I have directed Bible Schools and worked with children's reading programs.

Q: Who is your all-time favorite Old Testament character?

Patty Sleem: I like David a lot. His multi-faceted character is revealed in so many stories, such as the stories about

David and Saul, and about David and Bathsheba. David was an individual who lived life to the fullest, and yet he struggled to remain in a faithful relationship with God through his many successes and failures. I have enjoyed reading the stories about David and trying to find the lessons in his life that would apply broadly to all of our lives.

Q: **What are you writing now?**

Patty Sleem: I am writing the sequel to a book called *Back in Time*. It's the second book in a series about a lady minister who has made a career change to leave the business world for ministry. She has high expectations about a life of service when she leaves her well-paid career in the business world, but she finds that many people are reluctant to accept a woman in the pulpit. The series shows the main character, Maggie Dillitz, in many world spots as she unwittingly gets involved in murder mysteries and other situations.

Q: **Do you plan to write any other books like *What the Bible Says About...?***

171

Patty Sleem: I'm thinking about it. I am toying with the idea of developing a series with individual books tailored to specific subjects. In other words, there could be a book which compiles only quotations and sayings pertaining to "Wealth and Power," for example. The books might be shorter in length and smaller in size. I think people are seeking advice on how to live their lives, and they are interested in what the Bible says about values, relationships, and major life issues. People are so busy these days, and I like the idea of providing valuable advice in a short form which people can read quickly.

Q: Do you have a favorite verse of scripture?

Patty Sleem: I find myself thinking deeply about various verses from time to time. I love the passage from Corinthians defining love, and this book gave me a chance to showcase the fact that the Bible contains much great poetry.

Q: Do you have a favorite book of the Bible?

Patty Sleem: I suppose the book in which I have found the most practical advice is James. The book of James is a very short book in the New Testament which is packed with common sense and practical advice that can be applied in life situations. Although the Bible was written many centuries ago, it's advice is as relevant today as when it was written. Very few books can stand the test of time the way the Bible has.

Q: **If someone were unfamiliar with the Bible and wanted to read more, where would you recommend that that person begin in his Bible study?**

Patty Sleem: Most people would do well to begin by reading one of the Gospels--Matthew, Mark, Luke, or John--in the New Testament.

Q: **Do you think it's important that people read the Bible?**

Patty Sleem: The Bible is a gift from God and is a collection of inspired stories and advice. I like the Bible because it tells the unvarnished truth about human beings. The Bible contains stories of rape, incest, murder, greed, love, jealousy, loyalty, and many other matters. I have always liked the Bible because it doesn't sugarcoat anything. It presents human beings the way they really are, and it contains so much "plain talk" about how things really are. Books like Ecclesiastes and Job might seem a little depressing to us, but they reveal lessons about life experience which can benefit us. At its most basic level, the Bible is the most truthful and accurate book I know of, and everything I know from living my own life so far confirms what the Bible says. The Bible is truth, and it is wisdom.

ALSO BY PREP PUBLISHING

available from your favorite bookstore or
order online at www.prep-pub.com

BACK IN TIME
Patty Sleem

SECOND TIME AROUND
Patty Sleem

BIBLE STORIES FROM THE OLD TESTAMENT
Katherine Whaley

A GENTLE BREEZE FROM GOSSAMER WINGS
Gordon Beld

A GENTLE BREEZE FROM GOSSAMER WINGS
Gordon Beld
1-885288-07-7 $18.00 320 pages

Pol Pot was the Khmer Rouge leader whose reign of terror caused the deaths of up to 2 million Cambodians in the mid-1970s. He masterminded an extremist, Maoist-inspired revolution in which those Cambodians died in mass executions, and from starvation and disease. This book of historical fiction shows the life of one refugee from this era of genocide.

"A GENTLE BREEZE FROM GOSSAMER WINGS will warm your heart and stimulate your mind. Every Christian in America should read it. "
—Robert H. Schuller

BACK IN TIME
Patty Sleem 1-885288-03-4 $18.00

Even more than timely than when it was written, Sleem explores discrimination against women in the ministry. When Maggie Dillitz trades in her Harvard MBA and a lucrative career in the business world for a Yale Divinity School degree and a career in ministry, she expects relief from the competitive pressures of business and a life of satisfying service. What Maggie encounters is discrimination against women in ministry.

"Sleem provides an engrossing look at the discrimination faced by female ministers."
—*LIBRARY JOURNAL*

"Lots of contemporary issues in a plot that pulls readers through the pages."
—*THE BOOK READER*

BIBLE STORIES FROM THE OLD TESTAMENT
Katherine Whaley 1-885288-12-3 $18.00

Engaging storyteller Katherine Whaley tells familiar and not-so-familiar Bible stories in a style guaranteed to delight and inform. Most stories are brief. The book begins with the Creation and continues through the reign of Solomon. Even informed readers will enjoy the stories of Abraham, Cain and Abel, Jacob and David, Moses, Judges, Saul, and others. The villains have good in them, and the virtuous are imperfect. The author talks in plain language, with an enjoyable lack of moralizing.

"Katherine Whaley combines a lifelong study and devotion to scripture with a writer's gift and a storyteller's dramatic flair to fashion."
The Fayetteville Observer-Times

SECOND TIME AROUND
Patty Sleem 1-885288-00-X $25.00

Kathryn Haddad is a fortysomething, attractive, successful businesswoman in Macon, GA. She is happily married to fellow Harvard Business School graduate Stefan, and they appear to be the poster couple for Southern baby boomers. However, Kathryn finds herself in the classic triangle where she loves two men in different ways but chooses to remain with her husband. The book has been called "part spiritual fiction, part contemporary romance, part murder mystery-- all master storytelling in the best Southern writing tradition."

"Sleem has captured the essence of small town Southern life and the many layers of relationships one finds there. She weaves a picture of 'the way things are done' in small town politics and families.
—*Detroit DAILY NEWS*

To order by mail any of the titles shown, just send a check or money order or your credit card number for the total amount, plus $3.50 postage and handling, to PREP, 1110 1/2 Hay Street Fayetteville, NC 28305. If you have a question about any of our titles, feel free to e-mail us at preppub@aol.com and visit our website at www.prep-pub.com

Name: _____
Phone #: _____
Address: _____
E-mail address: _____
          Payment: ☐ Check   ☐ Visa
                ☐ MasterCard
Credit Card #: _____ ____
Expiration Date: _____ _____
☐ $16.00—BACK IN TIME. Patty Sleem
☐ $17.00—(paperback) SECOND TIME AROUND. Patty Sleem
☐ $25.00—(hard cover) SECOND TIME AROUND. Patty Sleem
☐ $18.00—A GENTLE BREEZE FROM GOSSAMER WINGS. Gordon Beld
☐ $18.00—BIBLE STORIES FROM THE OLD TESTAMENT. Katherine Whaley
☐ $14.95—WHAT THE BIBLE SAYS ABOUT... *Words that can lead to success and happiness* Patty Sleem

THE MISSION OF PREP PUBLISHING IS TO
PUBLISH BOOKS AND OTHER PRODUCTS WHICH
ENRICH PEOPLE'S LIVES AND HELP THEM
OPTIMIZE THE HUMAN EXPERIENCE. OUR
STRONGEST LINES ARE OUR JUDEO-CHRISTIAN
ETHICS SERIES AND OUR BUSINESS & CAREER
SERIES.